GIN & JUICE

GIN & JUICE

A GUIDE TO PARENTING

JEBEDIAH BLOOMSBURY
—LONDON—

1896

CONTENTS

ROYAL FOREWORD

By Her Majesty Victoria, by the grace of God, Queen of the United Kingdom of Great Britain and Ireland, Defender of the Faith, Empress of India and mother of nine

For the modern woman who wishes to 'have it all'—a husband, a family, a rewarding job as monarch of the world's most powerful country—the production and care of children is an enormously demanding business.

Questions of diet, discipline and (in the case of many European royal families) derangement are just some of the thorny issues raised by having children, and the wealth of information on these and other subjects can be overwhelming for a young parent.

So thank goodness for this magnificent instructional volume, which features chapters from the leading child-rearing experts at work today. I only wish it had been written when my own children were young ; if nothing else, its handy size and deceptive bulk make it an ideal missile with which to fell a recalcitrant footman, assassin or unruly two-year-old.

I cannot commend it highly enough and urge you to study it carefully.

CHAPTER 1

DOES MY BUMP LOOK BIG IN THIS CORSET?

BY THE MARQUIS OF SWINDON

—

PHILANTHROPIST

So you have fallen pregnant. For a married woman, this should be the happiest news of your life. (For an unmarried woman, I have nothing further to say to you, other than : "repent".)

You will no doubt be excited and relieved to have fulfilled the most important of your duties towards your husband, and I shouldn't wonder that your delicate female heart is filled with some trepidation about the daunting road ahead.

Rest assured : within these pages you will find all the information you need, from the changes your body will undergo during pregnancy to the proper way to approach a fashionable bishop to perform a christening.

One note before we begin. It has become conventional for books to contend that an expectant mother is embarking upon a wonderful, rewarding journey that will put her in touch with Nature and the very core of her womanhood. This is bilge of the most dangerous kind : pregnancy is a positively horrible business, on a par with having to read the works of Mr George Bernard Shaw without recourse to strong drink ; or visiting a hospital in Swindon and being obliged to dole out money to the parasitic malingerers within.

I have known many, many pregnant women, most but not all of them bearers of my own children, and I can say without fear of contradiction that they all hated the experience from Genesis to Revelations.

Good luck!

Swindon

ASSIST ME !
WHAT IS BEFALLING
MY PERSONAGE ?

G ROWING A CHILD INSIDE YOURSELF is a very cunning trick, and its difficulty is not to be underestimated. If you imagine yourself to be a conjuror, and your baby a bunny rabbit, you may get some sense of just how clever and wonderful is Mother Nature. Sadly, unlike a conjuror, human females are not equipped with a false bottom in their hat through which to whip out the little bundle of joy—although many have noted the similarities between a lady giving birth and a lady being sawn in half.

But let us not get bogged down in the arts of the illusionist, and turn instead to humanity's own daily magic trick : the miracle of new life. Pregnancy may be astonishing, but it is in equal measure beastly. Here are some of the nuisances you ought to prepare yourself for during the months of gravidity :

Morning Sickness : enemy of poise and pre-lunch gaiety
Stimuli or situations that may cause morning sickness include : tobacco smoke, tobacco being smoked by others, inferior Sauternes, a silly housemaid, certain sorts of kedgeree, the French.

An indecently enlarged décolletage
With possible attendant sensitivity in this area.

Feeling more emotional or womanly
You may find yourself even more irrational and easily discombobulated than is normal.

Sudden fits of temper
These are to be guarded against, as it has been quite well proved that inflamed passions or tempers during pregnancy can be transmitted to the baby and cause him to grow up a degenerate.

A Compulsion to eat bitumen
Or coal, if your budget allows.

A decrease in your appetite for your wifely obligations to your husband
Do not be disheartened if your husband turns to a servant, relation, actress, &c. in order to tide himself over. This is quite normal.

WHATEVER IS GOING ON DOWN THERE ?!

THE MYSTERIOUS AND ANCIENT ART of growing a baby inside your womanly receptacle explained :

AT ONE MONTH your baby resembles a summer pudding.

AT TWO MONTHS your baby would be able to hold its own in a physical dispute with most freshwater fish, including opponents up to the size of a salmon.

AT THREE MONTHS its feet, toes, ears and social station are detectable.

AT FOUR MONTHS your baby's moral courage should be fully formed.

AT FIVE MONTHS, the baby should be ready to try Armagnac. Do not give it Calvados.

AT SIX MONTHS the baby is still rather weedy.

AT SEVEN MONTHS your baby is ravenous and needs plenty of hearty food. Eat as much as you can stomach, focusing particularly on eggs, flour, potatoes and hay.

AT EIGHT MONTHS your baby is all but fully grown and should be able to recognise most of the common hymns. Play to it on the pianoforte and feel it kick in time.

AT NINE MONTHS, your baby is ready for birthing and should be encouraged to vacate your insides promptly, calmly and in an orderly fashion.

THE CORRECT DIET
DURING PREGNANCY

IT IS OF PARAMOUNT IMPORTANCE to remember that you are eating for two. If this seems daunting, imagine that you are an American. Your baby is concerned with nothing but eating and drinking ; in this regard, it may help to think of baby as being like a member of the working class. Baby, like the poor, is always with us ; and, unlike the poor, it cannot be put to work in the scullery or lime kiln in exchange for its three square meals a day.

"So how am I to intake the necessary nutrients to feed this ravenous beast within, for I am an Englishwoman of the right sort whose habits are as dainty as they are upstanding ?" you may be asking yourself.

Fortunately, thanks to the wonderful scientific discoveries of some very clever men, help is at hand for the modern mother. It comes in the form of SUPER-FOODS.

Fig. 1. *Super-Foods.*
Not to be confused with...

...Super-Natural Foods
which may disagree with
baby (and each other).

Certain foods are almost preternaturally rich in the right sort of nutritious goodness and an expectant mother who follows a strict regimen of eating these is certain to deliver a healthy, strong child—and without a great deal of fuss or expense. Therefore, be sure to eat at least five of these daily:

—TRIFLE

—VENISON

—COCAINE (sprinkled in warm milk or snorted)

—ESSENTIAL OILS such as sump

—ROUGH SHAG (to be enjoyed in pipe before bed)

Fig. 2. Nanny's Trifle. Rich in Vitamin Sherry.

—DOCTOR GREGOR MACGREGOR'S UNMENTIONABLE EMBROCATION AND AXEL GREASE (rub on to chest or raw poultry)

—CLARET (watered ; avoid the year 1878 as it may cause internal bleeding)

—LEAFY GREEN VEGETABLES in goosefat

—SWAN (broiled NOT roasted)

—PIGEON COMPOTE

Fig. 3. Pigeon Compost. Less tasty than Compote but still Super.

WHATEVER
AM I HAVING ?

F EAR NOT ! You are almost certainly bearing a human. Recent developments in *Protuberology* even allow us to predict which sort. While purists may favour the traditional gender-divining method of urinating on a midwife and waiting to see whether she turns pink or blue, the modern scientist has now achieved predictive sexing accuracy of over $40\frac{1}{3}$ per cent—simply by staring long and hard at the shape of your belly.[1]

Fig. 1.

Fig. 2.

GIRL

BOY

[1] Margin for error +/- 50 per cent.

Fig. 3.

BOYISH GIRL

Fig. 4.

GIRLISH BOY

Fig. 5.

OCTUPLETS

THE UTMOST SIGNIFICANCE OF THE RIGHT SORT OF NAME

IT HAS BEEN SCIENTIFICALLY PROVED that a child with an upright and noble name is up to $14\frac{1}{2}$ times more likely to achieve worldly success and become a person of impeccable moral character.

See if you can tell which of the following people is a Good Egg and which a Bad from their name alone :

a) The Right Reverend Albert King
b) Jimmy McBastard

ANSWER : Reverend King is the Bishop of Lincoln. Mr McBastard is a petty criminal from Glasgow.

a) Patience Goodcook
b) Lil O'Slatternly

ANSWER : Miss Goodcook gives out soup to the poor of the East End. Lil O'Slatternly gives out favours of an intimate nature to sailors in the East End.

a) Nelson Stoutfellow
b) Jean-Pierre Papin

ANSWER : You may be surprised to hear that Mr Stoutfellow is in fact the villain ; he is a confidence trickster from Abroad who operates under an assumed name. Given his Francophone tinge, Mr Papin is probably a dastardly person too, all things considered.

AS YOU CAN SEE, it is vital to label your child correctly. Choose one of the following names and there is every chance your child will do marvellously well in life :

BOYS	GIRLS
Albert	Victoria
Isambard	Waterloo
Nelson	Clapham Junction
Hardy	Trafalgar
W.G.	Nightbus
Ignatius	Patience
Clarence	Modesty
Edgar	Silence
Wayne	Rhododendrina

IN CONCEPTIO MEMORIAM†

THANKS TO THE INDEFATIGABLE SELF-PROMOTION and relentless child-fathering exploits of the noted Association footballer Mr D. Beckham of Leytonstone and Los Angeles, it has become modish of late to name a child after the place of his or her conception.

Consider these children, all of whose births were registered last year, as possible sources of inspiration :

Conservatory Jilcott-Brown
Aintree Racecourse Jackson
India Knight
Paddington Waiting-Room
Doncaster D'Arblay-Vishnu-Belcher
Weston-Super-Mare Hopkins
Raj Tinkington-Tock
Red Lion Wilson

† Additional research by Mrs Albert Hall Barnes-Wallace and Mrs Chesterfield Pinkney.

FINAL PREPARATIONS

Fig. 1. Fielding Practice
Ensure your staff are thoroughly drilled in close catching
as the big day approaches.

BEING A QUESTION PROMPTLY ANSWERED

WHERE CAN I MEET OTHERS WHO ARE EXPECTING A BABY ?

THE IMPENDING BIRTH OF A FIRST CHILD forces us to acknowledge that we expectant parents are all in the same boat—even though some of our fellow passengers might be in steerage.

A pregnant lady of the right sort suddenly discovers herself being spoken to in a familiar manner by people who are, to be frank, of not at all the same social standing. Perhaps she may find a hitherto deferential local tradesman eager to tell her that his wife is big with child ; or a forward housemaid may pipe up that a cousin of hers has got herself into trouble. One even hears of a funny little woman who sells heather door-to-door quite openly attempting to start a conversation about her own daughter being in the family way.

For many, this opportunity to interact with those of a different background imparts a warm, rather inspiring feeling of community spirit and the sense of our common humanity transcending such leaden earthly concerns as standing and wealth and class.

And the very best of luck to them.

Many other expectant parents, however, simply do not wish to go through the awkward business of dealing with the working class, and to these ladies and gentlemen one has no hesitation whatsoever in recommending the excellent New Christian Children's Teaching Society.

Your parish will very likely have weekly meetings where you can meet other like-minded parents-to-be safe in the knowledge that the riff-raff should be largely kept out. Below is a very small sample of the instructional and educational services the NCCTS provides.

PENETRATIO PER VAGINAM

Full and frank discussion of the most base and unvarnished mechanics of conception. For decency's sake, Latin terms will be used. Dictionaries available in the atrium.

NEWFOUND DIFFICULTIES IN USING THE COMMODE

Featuring an opportunity for husbands to sit in mortified horror as a female of their very recent acquaintance regales the assembled company with shockingly personal information about her trials and tribulations upon the water closet.

STRETCHING (THE BOUNDARIES OF CREDIBILITY)

Physical exercises and gyrations of the sort that would see one laughed off the playing fields of Eton, or indeed any other educational establishment worthy of the name. Claimed to be advantageous to the health of your baby. Undignified in the extreme.

THE APPARENT BELIEF THAT THE PREGNANT HUMAN FEMALE IS AMPHIBIOUS

Trenchant views on the advantages of trying to give birth to a baby under water, while listening to whales, shelling prawns, sitting in a rock pool, cuddling a halibut and other such aquatic tomfoolery. With guest lecturer Monsieur Jules Verne.

For companionship, comfort, advice and a guaranteed absence of the great unwashed, join the NCCTS today.

CHAPTER 2

THE AGONIES AND INDIGNITIES OF CHILDBIRTH

BY DR FOSTER GLOUCESTER,
SHIP'S DOCTOR AND REAR ADMIRAL
AND
MR HIGGS, BO'SUN

THE BUSINESS OF CHILDBIRTH is almost uncannily like the business of winning a battle at sea. It is self-evident that vast quantities of water are involved, as well as a great deal of screaming, loud noises, courage and grappling hooks and, in the case of the non-officer class, the consumption of a lot of rum. The key manoeuvre is to get your flagship out of your walled harbour with the minimum of fuss and into the clear water of the nursery and the expert care of the sawbones.

As you prepare to give birth, imagine you are one of the great English naval commanders of days gone by. Plan meticulously. Be brave and bold. Try not to get shot in the eye. Make sure those murky depths that are the parts of your anatomy below the Plimsoll line hold no surprises for you.

If you imagine your baby to be trapped in the Magellan Straits, pinned down by a well-armed Spanish fleet, and your midwife to be a small fighting force of Her Majesty's nimblest frigates, you will not go far wrong.

Remember the three Ps—Preparation, Planning, Panic (do not)—and you will soon be celebrating the launch of a fine little English jollyboat. God bless your womanly regions and all who sail in them.

—F. GLOUCESTER, MD
—HIGGS, BO'SUN

THE BIRTHING PLAN : SUREST DEFENCE AGAINST MISHAPS, FLAPPING & DISCOMBOBULATION

YOU ARE ABOUT TO EMBARK upon a daunting undertaking and it is impossible to overstate the importance of planning. Be sure that you can answer all of the following queries :

1. *Where in your home are you going to have your baby ? Has the whole wing been cleared ?*
2. *Have you thoroughly instructed Cook as to the meals she should prepare for the duration of your indisposition ?*
3. *Is your husband comfortable ?*
4. *How many servants will you require ?*
5. *In case of an emergency relocation, have you packed a small overnight trunk ?*
6. *Can fewer than four men carry it comfortably ?*
7. *Has your wet nurse been primed and pumped ?*
8. *Have you notified* The Times *of the birth ?*
9. *Have you enough muslin ?*
10. *Is your upper lip stiff ?*

NOTE : a small minority of progressive/dangerous women are opting for 'non-home births'. Quite why these females should wish to visit a hospital while in a delicate condition—and have their poop deck exposed to all and sundry—is a matter of some bafflement, but to these women I say : may God forgive you, and at least try to do it under a blanket.

THE OVERNIGHT BAG—A CHECK LIST

PACK AS YOU MIGHT for a convivial shooting party in the Highlands or a small tropical expedition. Useful items might include : chaise (longue), shoes (court), cleft stick, dressing table, occasional table, tide table, dinner service, hurricane lamp, hatstand, elephant gun and deck plimsolls (two pairs).

A BIRTHING PLAN FOR MEMBERS
OF THE LOWER ORDERS

IS IT POSSIBLE TO GIVE BIRTH AT YOUR PLACE OF WORK ? If your employer is especially generous you may be given the afternoon off work (unpaid) to have the child. This so-called 'maternity leave' is purely on a grace-and-favour basis and should not be taken as encouragement to slack off or overbreed.

A STATELY HOME BIRTH

AN AVERAGELY WELL-APPOINTED English country seat offers multitudinous options for the English country woman who wishes to give birth in unfettered communion with Nature, in the manner of the glorious wild nymphs of mythology or the southern Europeans of the present day. Here are some accepted locations in your grounds in which to deliver a child.

A GRECO-ROMAN FOLLY IN THE GROUNDS OF YOUR COUNTRY HOUSE :

Advantages : Natural light. Child can begin classical education early. Undignified screaming during labour need not disturb your neighbours.
Disadvantages : Indecency of naked statues could be upsetting. Pigeons.

BEHIND A HA-HA :

Advantages : Fresh air. Low cost. Some privacy.
Disadvantages : Vulnerable to changes in the weather. Vulnerable to unexpected visits by the local hunt.

A 'BIRTHING POOL'—A LAKE OR DECENT-SIZED DUCK POND SHOULD BE IDEAL :

Advantages : Water can be soothing, both physically and emotionally. Spare towels &c. can be rested safely on lily pads.
Disadvantages : Drowning. Predatory fish. (Not recommended during winter months if ice-skating is being practised.)

AT ONE WITH NATURE

BABY AHOY !

BY NOW YOUR CUSHIONS SHOULD BE PLUMPED, your servants' quarters aired and your chimney thoroughly swept. It is time to launch your infant craft upon the high seas of life. Hoist the rigging, lash midwife to the wheel and set a course for motherhood.

1. NAVAL GAZING
ASK THE CREW to conduct a final visual inspection in a dignified and respectful manner.

Fig. 1. Anchoring the windlass to the fo'c'sle.
Make sure your jib is correctly trimmed.

2. MAL DE MÈRE

ASSESS YOUR PRESENT DEGREE OF BODILY DISPLEASURE.
It is an unfortunate fact of life that childbirth smarts
quite uncomfortably. In the Navy, palliative care for
those in pain is a daily concern, although fortunately I
have yet to attend to a sailor who is about to give birth !
(Although this is not for want of examining the crew
down below at every opportunity.) Happily, a pregnant
woman is in many ways almost identical to a container
vessel, and thus my methods can be quite simply adopted
from the brig to the birthing deck.

LEVEL OF DISCOMFORT :
Mild rocking in the hull.
TREATMENT : Rum (small sips).

———

LEVEL OF DISCOMFORT :
Creaking and groaning amidships ; some nausea.
TREATMENT : Bite down on piece of wood.

———

LEVEL OF DISCOMFORT :
Holed down below ; waters everywhere.
TREATMENT : Sing sea shanty and eat dried
ship's biscuit.

———

LEVEL OF DISCOMFORT :
Hull severely breached ; baby imminent.
TREATMENT : Repel borders; man lifeboats.
Every man for himself.

3. THE ECSTASY OF BIRTH

*"I say, steady on."

4. KNOTS, LANDING

CONGRATULATIONS ! The little lugger has slipped its moorings and is tacking gently against the swell. All that remains is to tie off the bowline.

5. BABYGROW HO !

YOU MAY NOW SIGNAL the happy news to those who have chosen to remain ashore (or in the library, smoking).

It's a girl !   *It's a buoy !*

TESTING A NEWBORN

WITHIN A MINUTE OR TWO OF BIRTH, your physician will perform a series of tests upon your issue, scoring the child two, one or *nul points* on each to give a total.

—Upper lip is stiff.
—Buttercup held under chin ; does not flinch or cry.
—Responds alertly upon recitation of a georgic.
—Nose is wet, coat shiny.
—Look of distaste when shown picture of
  a Continental carrying on in an overly
  emotional manner.
—Grasps miniature cricket bat.
—Only one head.
—Recognises colours of some of the better
  public schools.
—Does not have evil look in eye.
—Blood is blue, urine green.
—Screaming lustily, is quiet when told.

Competition is the *sine qua non* of healthy child development, and there is simply no sense in dillydallying and allowing your newborn to fall behind in the race of life. Tot up your child's score.

20-24 : Your child is sure to be a most
           splendid success.
15-19 : There may yet be a place for him at
           a minor public school.
10-14 : Perhaps she will be a sweet-natured girl.
  0-9 : Export child to colonies without delay.

In the event of an entirely POINTLESS child, additional examinations may be required :

OBSERVATION № 1.
NON-JOCULAR OCULAR OVULARITY

—

CAREFULLY MEASURE DISTANCE BETWEEN EYES FOR INDICATIONS OF MORAL TORPOR

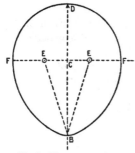

*Fig. 1. Narrow venting.
Risk of pusillanimity.*

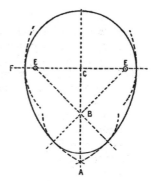

*Fig. 2. Widely pimped.
Some dissembling likely.*

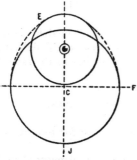

*Fig. 3. Single eye to middle
of forehead. May require
monocle.*

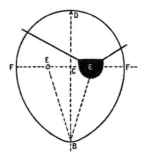

*Fig. 4. Black eyepatch.
Check for parrot droppings.*

OBSERVATION № 2.
NON-PARTICULAR FOLLICULAR FUNICULARITY
—

**SLOWLY EXAMINE SHAPE OF HEAD TO DETERMINE
MAXIMUM INTELLECTUAL CAPACITY**

Fig. 1. Redeeming features :

(*a*) *Golden Mean*   (*b*) *London Orbital*   (*c*) *Marble Arch*
     30 *fl. oz.*   3½ *quarts*   2 *fingers*

Fig. 2. Non-redeeming features :

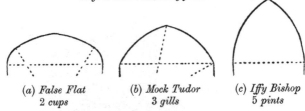

(*a*) *False Flat*   (*b*) *Mock Tudor*   (*c*) *Iffy Bishop*
     2 *cups*   3 *gills*   5 *pints*

COMMON CLASSIFICATIONS
Pointless child with minor cranial crenellation : *gooseberry fool*
Pointless child with Mock-Tudor presentation : *village idiot*
Pointless child with pointy head : *oxymoron*

OBSERVATION № 3.
WIND SPEED

1. *Breezy Burp*   2. *Blustery Bot*   3. *Gale-force Guff*

THE ROLE OF THE FATHER IN ALL THIS

UNTIL QUITE RECENTLY, the business of childbirth was exclusively woman's work, as much a female dominion as commerce, politics and reason are the preserve of man. Of course these days, things have changed quite drastically and many men are keen to be involved in the process at every level.

Thus, there is now absolutely no reason why the modern papa should not write his wife a letter of encouragement in the days leading up to the birth.

BEING A QUESTION PROMPTLY ANSWERED

TWINS : WHAT TO DO IN A TWO-DO ?

THE FIRST ORDER OF BUSINESS is to discern which is the Good Twin and which the Evil. This should be accomplished without much difficulty by studying the faces of the children and searching for clues—such as a kindly (or cruel) look in the eye ; smooth, pleasant skin (or cryptic Satanic numbers etched into the skull &c.) and a readiness to smile politely (or glare in rage as dark passions bubble in the infant breast).

If you cannot say with certainty that one of your babies is born in the Light and one is possessed of a black nature, it may be that both siblings are fundamentally balanced of temperament. Well done to all concerned. Now it is a simple matter of picking your favourite and treating each baby accordingly.

As they grow older, encourage healthy competition between the twins by always giving one a slightly better toy, marginally larger portion of food and subtle but unmistakably differing amounts of care and affection. Twins who are not warring can unite to form a very dangerous alliance, and it is for this reason that you ought never to leave them alone together.

Although the drawbacks to twin-rearing are legion, comfort yourself with the knowledge that twins can be tremendous earners of money if they are sufficiently pleasing on the eye to pose for *photolumière* plates in periodicals ; appear in the circus ; or submit themselves to scientific experimentations.

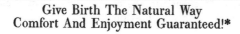

CHAPTER 3

BECOMING ACQUAINTED WITH YOUR BABY

BY LADY TRACY HOGGSWALLOP
—
HORSE WHISPERER

CATHERINE THE GREAT
EMPRESS AND AUTOCRAT OF ALL THE RUSSIAS

YOUR BABY. Most precious little bundle on God's green earth. Treasure trove of infinite delights and potentialities. Almost impossible to hold a conversation with. Such is the wonder and devilry of the baby.

Like the Parisian waiter, who can of course speak English perfectly well but selectively pretends otherwise, the baby can appear quite unable to communicate in our language. This is not the case—you simply need to know what the baby's signs and signals mean, as well as the cues to which baby will respond.

My inspiration has long been my great-grandmother, Chardonnay Hoggswallop-Stravinsky, who first formulated the principles of 'horse whispering' and who was the *de facto* right hand of Catherine the Great of Russia. Chardonnay was the subject of a great scandal in the popular press at the end of the last century ('Bonkers Ruskie's Dobbin Shame—And Brit Toff Is Randy Nag Madam') but I have made it my life's work to rehabilitate her reputation, and apply her methods to both equine and human youngsters.

As the years have gone by, and I continue to be unjustly disbarred from practising as a veterinarian, I have concentrated on applying Chardonnay's principles mainly to humans. The parent who can look at baby from just the right angle, reassure it, hold its gaze, blow up its nostrils and give it a carrot is already a great way down the path of meaningful communication with the child.

Tracy

PRACTICALITIES : THE RUDIMENTS OF BABY HANDLING

PROPERLY HANDLED, a small child may bring many years of pleasure. You may find it useful to familiarise yourself with the more common disciplines of child-rearing for those rare occasions when the household staff are unavailable or Nanny is indisposed.

1. HOLDING BABY

Grasp securely at arm's length, with head upright and toes pointing to floor (reversed in the southern hemisphere).

2. CHANGING BABY

First locate the guilty party.

Suitably attired, slowly approach your subject. Use of a canary
should alert you to any dangerous build-up of gases.

Bottom Boom.
Your canary is clearly faulty. Replace both bird and baby
before the next nappy change.

3. CLEANING BABY

Place in tub and scrub vigorously. Use a dash of lemon or
vinegar behind the ears, taking care not to over-marinate.

Rinse and wring. More robust children may benefit
from one or two passes through the laundress's mangle.

Once dressed, baby should be placed outside and aired
until dry to the touch.

COOING OR MOOING ? RECOGNISING THE CRIES OF AN INFANT

A RCANE AND MYSTERIOUS TO THE LAYPERSON they may be, but to the trained baby handler, the cries of the young human are as full of meaning and clear in purpose as a display of sexual readiness from an engorged peacock or a show of territorial aggression from a superstrength kestrel.[1]

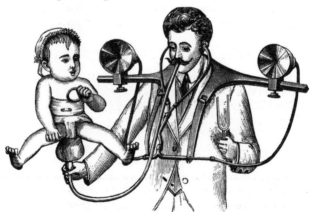

Fig. 1. *Call and Response : a researcher tunes his latest subject to the key of E minor, believed to be the tonal range favoured by nutcrackers worldwide.*

---

[1] I am indebted to my eminent colleague Dr Cuthbert Clarice-Starling, ornithologist and author of *The Corvid Within* : *What Jackdaws Can Teach Us About Child Development* for advice on this subject.

LISTEN CAREFULLY to the sounds emanating from the farthest reaches of your house and attend to, or ignore, the child accordingly.

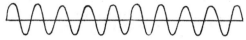

HIGH-PITCHED CRY, RISING AND FALLING IN VOLUME
Denotes that baby may be hungry.

SHRILL, RAPID SQUEALS ACCOMPANIED BY GASPING
AND SHAKING OF FISTS
Denote that baby may have spotted a parlourmaid purloining the best silverware from the sideboard.

THROATY WARBLING CRY REMINISCENT OF THE
CHAFFINCH OR THROATY WARBLER
Denotes that baby may be thirsty, or that it may have swallowed a bird.

DIRGE-LIKE DRONE REMINISCENT OF 'GOD SAVE THE
QUEEN' ACCOMPANIED BY SALUTING MOTIONS WITH HAND
Denotes that baby may be feeling patriotic.

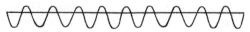

LOW-PITCHED, GASPING CRY WITH REDDENING OF
THE FACE
Denotes that baby may be ashamed, possibly as a result of having caught sight of its own ankles.

SPEAKING TO BABY : THE MIRACLE OF SIGN LANGUAGE

SHOULD YOUR CHILD HAVE FAILED to grasp the rudiments of English or Latin within its first few months then do not despair. For help is, in the most literal sense, at hand. Thanks to recent advances in the realm of DIGITAL COMMUNICATIONS it is now possible to converse clearly and precisely with infants of all ages.

STEP 1.
ENSURE BABY is within range and commence gesticulation. If reception is poor you may need to increase your signal strength or adjust baby's position.

FIG. 1. NOT WAVING, BUT FROWNING.

STEP 2.
INITIATE SMALL TALK. Using simple words will put baby
at ease.

One   *Two*   *Five*

Rabbit   *Beef*   *Rabbit with
Beef*

STEP 3.
ONCE BABY has mastered the essentials of non-verbal
reasoning you may move on to more abstract discourse,
although controversial subjects such as the Irish Question
should be avoided close to bedtime.

*Mummy has
a headache*

*Father is
hoping for a
Conservative
government*

*Aunt Agatha
wears a
wooden leg*

SPEAKING TO OTHER MOTHERS : THE INSPIRING TECHNOLOGICAL AND SOCIAL REVOLUTION THAT IS MATERS-NET

EXHAUSTION. Feelings of despair. Uncomfortable chaffing. These are but a few of the trials and tribulations facing the young mother, and hitherto they have most likely been burdens to be borne quite alone.

Thanks to the splendid imagination and dedication of a group of ladies in Clapham, this may be changing for ever. In July of 1895, while they were both nursing tiny infants, a Mrs Blackwell and her dear friend Mrs Pottington were sorry to find their regular perambulations on the Common curtailed owing to their being too busy overseeing the care of their babes.

"Had we been working class, we might have simply shouted at one another over the garden fence," says Mrs Blackwell with a laugh.

"Of course, we are NOT working class," interjects Mrs Pottington hastily.

Mrs Blackwell continues : "It was impossible for us to get away from all the duties of hearth and home that are the lot of the new mother, so we happened upon the idea of sending carrier pigeons to each other bearing helpful recipes, cheerful messages and other friendly communications."

However, this excellent scheme suffered a drawback.

"We had one pigeon, Albert, who was most reliable and would fly straight as an arrow," explains Mrs Blackwell. "But the other, Sooty, was quite erratic and would often miss his intended roof, or peck his messages out of his little pigeon satchel in an act of defiance."

"An excellent recipe for Cocoa Flummery was lost for ever thanks to Sooty's wicked waywardness," adds Mrs Pottington with some bitterness.

It was then that the two friends hit upon a solution that would not have shamed one of the great engineers of the railways.

"I erected a large wire mesh on the roof of my house in which to entrap the ill-disciplined pigeon at the culmination of his journeys," says Mrs Blackwell. "And misdirected avian communications were soon a thing of the past."

Within weeks, several other mothers in the area were also using pigeons and nets to communicate and share experiences. Mrs Pottington turned her gazebo into a small factory to manufacture the pigeon-entrapping lattices, Mrs Blackwell distributed them among the young mothers of Clapham, and Maters-Net was born.

"It has grown at a remarkable rate," says Mrs Blackwell. "From just us two friends, we now have a network of several thousand ladies in the suburbs of southern London, all sending out carrier pigeons with messages and trapping them in nets, the better to discuss and share the daily burden of bringing up baby."

Indeed, the fame of Maters-Net has so grown that the Prime Minister recently invited Mrs Pottington, Mrs Blackwell and several of the Mater-Netters to tea. Sadly, the Right Honourable Gentleman was quite badly mauled by a pigeon, to say nothing of the treatment meted out to him by the ladies, and he has had to retire from public life as a result.

WOULD YOU ADJUDGE MY BEHAVIOUR CAPRICIOUS, HEADSTRONG OR OTHERWISE IN CONTRAVENTION OF ORDINARY SOUND THINKING ?

AMONG THE MANY INNOVATIONS of Maters-Net has been to provide a forum for ladies to air their private grievances. A Maters-Net mater may send a pigeon out to her fellows and be guaranteed a fair and forthright assessment of her difficulty—be it one involving a domestic servant, a question of etiquette or even relations with her husband. Given the degree of anonymity involved in the pigeon-and-net method of communication, it is possible for quite full and frank exchanges of views to take place without the awkwardness that such robust conversation can provoke in day-to-day life. So, if you should find yourself wrestling with a dilemma or stewing over a perceived injustice, simply write down your problem and attach it to a pigeon, marking it *Would You Adjudge My Behaviour Capricious, Headstrong Or Otherwise In Contravention Of Ordinary Sound Thinking* ? Or employ the handy time-saving acronym WYAMBCHOOICOOST.

BABY BOASTING

For any new parent, especially with a first child, meeting other parents can be a most reassuring experience. It is often of great comfort to know that others are experiencing similar concerns and to be able to share anecdotes. Primarily, however, it is enjoyable to make other people feel inadequate about their child's development *vis à vis* one's own progeny's.

Perhaps a conversation might begin in which an acquaintance should say : "Of course, little Samuel is already grabbing." No matter that your own boy of the same age simply lies on his back gurgling in the manner of a simpleton ; the correct response is : "How wonderful—I remember when young Bartholomew began grabbing. Of course, he has now progressed to simple juggling and uttering his first tentative phrases in Hungarian."

Or it may be that a friend with a child born in the same month as your own should make proud reference to her darling Jack's prodigious smiling. This is an ideal opportunity for you to say : "And you must be so very thrilled. Of course, Joshua has already accepted a commission in the Coldstream Guards. We are so excited—the General believes him to be quite the most advanced ten-month-old they have yet seen."

Remember : life is a competitive game, and any slight advantage—real, or entirely invented—should be shoved down the throats of one's rivals without hesitation.

BEING A QUESTION PROMPTLY ANSWERED

TIT OR TEAT ?

OF THE MANY FRACTIOUS DEBATES about the practicalities and ethics of juvenile human husbandry, none is more keenly contested than the question of whether to feed baby from the breast or the bottle. Here, the advantages of each are summarised :

THE BREAST :
Mother can form a bond during feedings—especially if she engages the wet nurse in pleasant small talk while the woman is suckling the child.

Many of the essential foodstuffs that baby needs are already present in the wet nurse, or can be inserted into her by Cook.

A reasonably well-maintained wet nurse should be sterile and free from germs.

Via contact with the wet nurse, your baby may build up antibodies to the poor.

THE BOTTLE :
Allows the expressing of milk if you are going somewhere where it is impractical to whip out a wet nurse—for instance, the opera, a lecture on unusual pottery or a bare-knuckle boxing match.

Frees mother up for the more important aspects of motherhood, such as choosing a school and making sure child has a book on its head to improve posture.

Reduces risk of child forming a bond with wet nurse. This lessens the possibility of upset if wet nurse is summarily dismissed from household for suspected theft, or for attempted suspected theft.

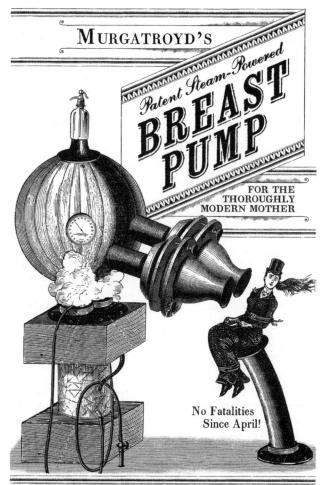

CHAPTER 4

THE IMPORTANCE
OF
ROUTINE

BY MISS GERTRUDE FJORD-METTÖD

—

ASSISTANT SUPERINTENDENT (1883–1885)
NORWEGIAN NATIONAL ORPHAN BARN
AND PETTING ZOO

MISS FJORD-METTÖD COMFORTS
A YOUNG MOTHER

B ABIES ARE BY THEIR NATURE IRASCIBLE, unruly, ill-disciplined and extremely noisy. In this regard, they are strikingly similar to foreigners. However, much in the way that Her Majesty's Armed Forces have subdued natives around the globe, so can the parent force the child to submit to her will.

Our cousins in Norway have made quite remarkable advances in the field of infant husbandry via theory, laboratory work and experimentation, some of them scrupulously ethical and some of them less so. They firmly encourage the absolute primacy of routine, and I am in complete agreement. Here, I present an abridged extract from my book *Timekeeping, Discipline and the Switch* : *Bringing Up Baby the Fjord-Mettöd Way* (Morten Harket Press, 1895).

There has been some heated debate in ladies' periodicals and chattering rooms about my techniques and a lot of wishy-washy rot spouted about allowing children to 'express themselves' and 'develop at their own rate'. I expect these same women would attempt to stew a partridge without using a recipe book ; or try to remove the creature's innards with an insufficiently sharp knife ! I make no pleasantry whatsoever when I say that caring for a young baby is every bit as grim, messy and unrewarding as butchering game, and, unlike a dead partridge, a baby can give one a nasty nip. Treat it firmly and with caution.

—FJORD-METTÖD

THE FJORD-METTÖD METHOD

RIGID ADHERENCE to this simple regimen will ensure sound sleep, even temper, good digestion and general contentment ; and it may conceivably be advantageous for the child as well.

Five o'clock   Rise. Drink a large cup of hot, sweet tea. Return to your bedchamber while a wet nurse administers the first feed of the day.

A quarter past Five   Nanny arrives. Scold Nanny thoroughly for her unacceptably late start to the day's work. Eat a Jugged Hare.

Six o'clock   If your nanny is from India, Malaya or Lancashire, accuse her of stealing from the household. Drink a glass of tepid water with snuff in it.

Seven o'clock   Go out for a day's riding, shooting or, if in Town, perambulation and socialising.

A half-past Six that evening   The child's time with Mater and Pater. Children treasure this family time with their parents, and it is most vital for their development.

Thirty-two minutes past Six   Have Nanny put the child to bed. Drink an enormous glass of gin, with gin in it.

FIG. 1. FJORD FOCUS
FOLLOWING THE METHOD

FIG. 2. FJORD TRANSIT
NOT FOLLOWING THE METHOD

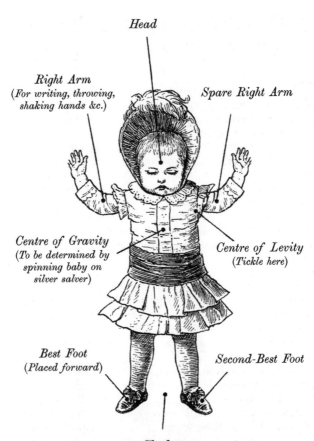

Head

Right Arm
(*For writing, throwing, shaking hands &c.*)

Spare Right Arm

Centre of Gravity
(*To be determined by spinning baby on silver salver*)

Centre of Levity
(*Tickle here*)

Best Foot
(*Placed forward*)

Second-Best Foot

Shadow
(*May not be present during bouts of cradle cap or vampirism*)

THE FJORD MODEL BABY : AN OWNER'S MANUAL

BABY'S THREE DISTINGUISHING CHARACTERISTICS ARE : attempting to perform tasks beyond its capabilities (smiling, walking) ; making a lot of noise ; and costing a great deal of money.

One of the most dangerous myths about baby is that of the 'first smile'. Many young parents attach a great amount of emotional significance to the occasion upon which their child smiles at them for the first time. O, naïve, feeble heart !

The smile-like grimace of a nursing baby is now thought to be a result of wind trapped inside the infant, and it only goes to prove how vulgar children are that they might derive humour or enjoyment from such a personal and delicate bodily malfunction.

On the other hand, some scientists believe that the infant may be smiling in recognition of a parent. Such behaviour is a very slippery slope which could, if left unchecked, lead to the child attempting in time to converse with its mother or father without first being spoken to.

Be it a function of digestive incorrectness or a primitive attempt at unprompted communication, it is clear that the 'smile' is a gateway to all manner of unsuitable behaviour. Be always vigilant for any signs of your child smiling at you ; if you suspect the baby may be about to smile, turn away quickly and cover its pen with a cloth.

Baby's efforts to walk are similarly unimpressive. Note well its unsteady gait and listing balance as it teeters and careens around like an Irishman on pay-day.

A Rum Tot. More weaving than a Dundee jute mill.

For decency's sake, do not be seen in public with baby until it can at least sit up straight without tethering.

In addition to its blundering attempts to perambulate, baby can be noisy in the extreme, babbling and squawking with a total disregard for decorum. Fortunately, baby tends toward guilelessness and will very likely not notice if you put in some ear plugs.

Be aware that baby can be an enormous drain on a household's financial resources. If you think of baby as a large pit into which to pour your hard-earned (or hard-inherited) money, you will not go far wrong. The only hope is that it may become wealthy in later life ; if so, you should invoice it in full for the food, care, &c. it received in its early years.

Finally, recognise that looking directly at baby is the worst mistake a parent can make. Eye contact with baby can cause : anxiety, a lack of physical and moral courage, astigmatism, the debilitating condition Jellyfishing of the Spine, deviancy, smiling. Resist the temptation at all cost ; if you are still minded to gaze upon your progeny, ensure that either you or the infant are securely blindfolded.

GETTING BABY'S MEASURE

IT IS NEVER TOO EARLY to feel anxious about how your child compares to an arbitrary set of targets.

WEIGHT

BABY SHOULD BE WEIGHED every other day (or daily when the moon is waxing). Where a public weighbridge is employed you may find it beneficial to clear the area of livestock first.

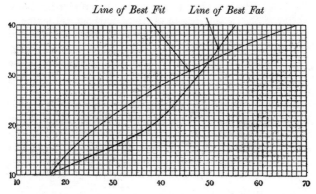

Line of Best Fit   *Line of Best Fat*

Once assayed, baby may be assigned to one of four official classifications, as determined by the Parliamentary Weights & Measures Act (1889) :

0 *to* $\frac{1}{5}$ AIN'T-SHE-DAINTY ?
$\frac{1}{5}$ *to* $\frac{1}{3}$ BANTAMWEIGHT
$\frac{1}{3}$ *to* $\frac{2}{3}$ FILLING-OUT-NICELY
$\frac{2}{3}$ *to* $\frac{3}{4}$ FREAKSHOW

LENGTH

INFANTS should be measured in the Reed-Barnard Position (face down, one leg raised). Where relevant, results should be trade-weighted and seasonally adjusted.

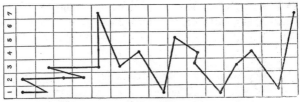

Rebased to 112 on alternate Tuesdays.

The ideal graph will bear a striking resemblance to the profile of the Alps (as viewed from *Langnau*). A graph that resembles the Alps as seen from the Italian side is acceptable, but leaves room for improvement. In the event of a Pyrenean graph contact your physician or travel agent immediately.

DENSITY

NURSLING DENSITY is a product of weight x length x pie. Particularly dense infants may require a reduction in nutritional intake or a new governess.

One Pie   *Two Pies*   *All The Pies*

SETTING BABY TO WORK

WHATEVER AGE YOUR OFFSPRING, it should be in a position to make a positive contribution to the health and wealth of your household.

FIG. 1. IN THE PARLOUR

FIG. 2. AT THE DINNER PARTY

FIG. 3. AT ONE'S CLUB

FIG. 4. ON THE GLORIOUS TWELFTH

THE DISTRESSED INFANT : MORTAL ENEMY OF RESTFULNESS AND MATERNAL GAIETY

IF YOU HAVE FOLLOWED the Fjord-Mettöd Method assiduously, you will have experienced few difficulties with your baby, who should by now be sleeping through the night, reading simple Latin, holding its tongue and generally being a colourful and correct little thread in society's rich tapestry.

However, it is a regrettable fact that some—only a few, but some—children nevertheless continue to present signs of wilfulness well into their first year of life, no matter how firmly my Method has been applied. Are these children simply born Evil ? Is there some deficiency in their parents' stock ? Is an international Leftist conspiracy somehow to blame ? These are questions for others more qualified than I, for I am a mere baby expert with decades of experience who knows far more about children than any of the lily-livered nincompoops who presume to disagree with me.

If baby is still crying in the night, breaking wind or smiling despite your best efforts, do not despair. Assuming that you are fortunate enough to have a reasonable-sized house, simply leave the baby in one of the distant wings until it sees the error of its ways. If you have both a town and country residence, bamboozle the baby into submission by moving between the two several times a week. A certain amount of separation anxiety is to be expected during the first few weeks of

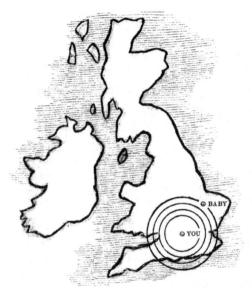

Fig. 1. *Quite Close Enough*

this programme, but you should be able to take your mind off things by reading a book or playing canasta. In any respect, by the age of three, the child will be ready to attend public school and your woes will be over.

THE LOWER ORDERS

IF YOU ARE UNFORTUNATE to be not only working class but also in possession of a noisy baby, I can only offer my condolences. Try to put the infant's name down for one of the better workhouses without delay. Perhaps consider not breeding in future, dedicating your attentions instead to gambling, gin and the music hall and other pastimes better suited to your social station.

BEING A QUESTION PROMPTLY ANSWERED

CAN FOREIGNERS TEACH US ANYTHING ABOUT BRINGING UP CHILDREN ?

"SURELY NOT!" the well-bred English reader will cry. "After all, they have yet to invent the railway locomotive, the pre-prandial libation or the concept of saying the opposite of what one means for the preservation of social decorum."

Au contraire : splendid work is being done in the Mystic East in the field of child control. In her excellent primer *Battleaxe : My Mother the Tiger*, the estimable Oriental parenting expert Mrs Syko Ma has demonstrated just how effective daily twenty-three-hour sessions of violin practice can be in the training of child violinists. Her entirely sensible recommendation of refusing to feed a child until it can play Tchaikovsky's Violin Concerto in D major from start to finish has ensured that the salons of Peking echo to the sound of perfectly played symphonies and concerti, although the problem of feral infant violinists escaping and stealing food from local restaurants is an unfortunate side effect.

Her methods of dealing with a six-month-old child who scores only 99 out of 100 in its Advanced Calculus studies may not be to the taste of some gentler hearts, but there are others who feel that being locked in the attic until one is twenty-six would provide one with an ideally peaceful place in which to concentrate on schoolwork.

So what else can we learn from these Asiatic masters of youngster husbandry ? A recent programme between the Kowloon Centre for Child-rearing & Coal-mining and Trinity College Cambridge Heath attempted to shed light on their methods. In the spirit of cultural exchange, eighteen English children were sent to live in China. Unhappily, little useful data could be gathered from their stay as the visiting children had been brought up to speak only when spoken to, and none of their hosts could speak English. This made for a rather uneventful six-year stay, but some of the subjects became quite acceptable *mah-jong* players.

Their Chinese counterparts were taken from the Orient, brought to live in England and put under a strict regimen of hearty meals, sitting up straight and playing Battledore and Shuttlecock at the Fjord-Mettöd Educational Centre (Holloway Prison campus). Unfortunately, they all escaped, adding weight to the worrying reports emanating from far-flung bits of the Empire that the Chinese are both immensely clever and possessing of firm views about the best way to play badminton.

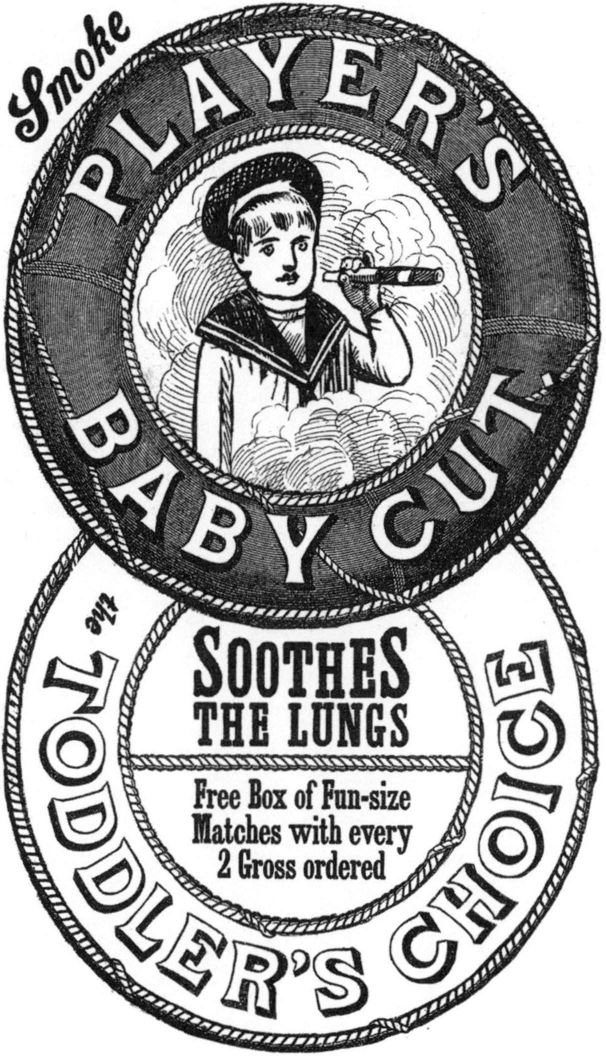
Smoke
PLAYER'S
BABY CUT.
the
TODDLER'S CHOICE
SOOTHES
THE LUNGS
Free Box of Fun-size
Matches with every
2 Gross ordered

CHAPTER 5

THE NURSERY YEARS

BY MISS JOLETTINA FORBES-FROSTE

—

ÜBER-NANNY-IN-CHIEF TO THE
OTTOMAN CALIPHATE

MISS FORBES-FROSTE ENJOYS A RELAXING STROLL
IN THE CALIPH'S GARDENS

I T HAS BEEN THIRTY-FIVE YEARS now since I undertook my first assignment as a nanny. My calling has taken me all over the British Empire, and into the uncivilised world as well, to care, to coach and, if occasion demands, to crush. I estimate that I have supervised the children of over 250 families—and never a conviction yet.

The question I am most often asked (other than "Have you considered professional wrestling?") is : "Have you ever found yourself at your wits' end with a child's behaviour ?" To this I say simply : "Absolutely not. The whole dog-and-pony show is an complete travesty since they got rid of my dear friend 'Stone Cold' Viscount Austin" ; and "Not thus far—but I will never do child actors, royalty or the offspring of progressive types in the fashionable bits of north London."

I have yet to be defeated by a child, no matter how recalcitrant, and I am delighted to share my methods with you in this chapter. In short : speak softly, and carry a big stick. Or, better yet, a blunderbuss.

Jo H

CARING FOR YOUR CHILD : DO NOT TRY THIS AT HOME

IN WHICH MISS JOLETTINA FORBES-FROSTE FURNISHES THE YOUNG MOTHER WITH HER VIEWS ON THE RELATIVE MERITS OF ENGAGING A PROFESSIONAL SO THAT A WOMAN MIGHT 'RETURN TO WORK', AGAINST THE AMATEUR'S SPIRITED BUT SHAMBOLIC ATTEMPTS TO CARE FOR HER OWN CHILD, THIS BEING A JUICY DEBATE MARBLED THROUGHOUT WITH STRONGLY HELD OPINIONS

A WORD OF CAUTION : my nannying techniques were not formulated overnight, nor were their secrets easily won. Herewith but three examples from my personal experience. Ask yourself if you think that an untrained mother could have handled each situation with the calm authority of a professional nanny.

IN THE FLESHPOTS of the *Cap d'Antibes*, where I cared for the children of the disgraced Count of Rotterdam, I devised my famed HOUSE RULES, a unique combined system for the quietening of noisy infants and the playing of *punto banco*.

I expect you would have lost all your money at roulette. And now you wish to gamble just as carelessly with your child's future.

———

ON THE IMPOSING PLAINS of Outer Mongolia, where I was nanny to the most powerful khan of his day, I had to face down a toddler-led spate of horse-rustling. Only by exiling the offender to 'The Naughty Steppes' did I quell the uprising.

What would you have done ? Fled in tears to the Hindu Kush and blamed the child's behaviour on excitement-engendering orange barley water ?

IN THE WILDS of Southern Africa, only quick thinking and the suggestion that "we all take a moment to calm down and think about what we have done" saved me from an untimely casserole-related death at the hands of a local chief upset with my firm handling of his first-born.

Try looking after your precious baby when you are being sautéed with papaya.

With thousands of professionals available at reasonable rates, it never ceases to amaze and dismay that anyone of any means whatsoever should attempt to care for their own child. Let me be perfectly clear :
Nanny. Knows. Best.

In the interests of fairness, the case for Remaining At Home With Baby will be advanced by Mrs Angina Phelps, mother of nine and author of 'Woman—Hold Your Tongue and Leave the Professional Arena to the Men : Why Working Mothers Must Be Stopped'

Modern mothers can be divided into two categories. The first believes firmly that her sole purpose in life is to nurture and care for her child, never letting it out of her sight until the offspring is itself married (in the case of a girl) or making its way in the world (in the case of a boy). These mothers are referred to in the literature of child-rearing as bear mothers, utterly devoted to their offspring and fiercely protective in their constant vigilance thereof.

The other type of mother gives birth and, practically as soon as the mite has been propelled from her womb, sets about preparing for her 'Return to Work'. With not a thought for the damage to the child, she engages the services of multifarious nannies and 'baby-sitters', at considerable expense mind you, so she can go back to her so-called 'work', often as an assistant to a confidence trickster, free-lance harlotry or even, in some of the vilest cases, in the Law. These we shall refer to as SNAKE MOTHERS, so named for their amorality, their greed and, experts believe, the slithery scales they keep hidden under their shamefully modern petticoats.

The new mater who had previously enjoyed pretensions to a career need decide only this : will she be a kindly and protective BEAR MOTHER who gives her darling every care and attention she can ; or a SNAKE MOTHER who abandons her infant to the tender mercies of a stranger just to satisfy her own vanity and ambition ?

MISS JOLETTINA FORBES-FROSTE ADDS : Shortly after writing this article, remain-at-home-mater Mrs Phelps was sadly driven quite mad by the incessant shouting of her children and had to be committed to a sanatorium. I hate to say : "I told you so."

METTLE DETECTION :
THE ART OF CHOOSING
THE RIGHT NANNY

HOW, THEN, IS ONE TO CHOOSE A NANNY, that vital cog in the machinery of a child's development ? Thankfully, the days of pairing off potential child-minders in a grisly fight to the death armed only with an array of children's cutlery have long since passed, although a brief arm-wrestling contest may still help the discerning employer to eliminate one or two of the feebler candidates. Instead, the modern mistress of the house will employ an artful blend of close questioning and keen visual inspection to make her natural selection.

Fig. 1. *Two young nannies contest a position in less enlightened times. Limited edition prints available.*

EXERCISE 1.

APPLYING YOUR SKILLS OF SCRUTINY AND DEDUCTION, examine each applicant in turn and determine which is the Nanny, the Ninny and the Hey-Nonny-No.

CANDIDATE A
MISS TICKLE

CANDIDATE B
MISS ADVENTURE

CANDIDATE C
MISS MOSS

Likes : *Hot summer nights. The feel of leather against skin. Champagne.*

Dislikes : *Children*

Likes : *Fresh mountain air. The thrill of the climb. Milking goats.*

Dislikes : *Dresses*

Likes : *An orderly nursery. The pride of a job well done. Buttered tea cakes.*

Dislikes : *Untidiness*

The correct answer is D, or NONE OF THE ABOVE. Miss Tickle is a HOOTERNANNY with designs upon your husband of the basest kind. Miss Adventure is a MANNYNANNY—she schemes to seduce your nursemaid or elope with the parlour girl. While Miss Moss is evidently a SUFFRAGIST and will have thrown herself under your horse before the week is out.

THE NURSERY : A ROOM TO SET YOUR CHILD UPON THE PROPER PATH

ENVIRONMENT MAKETH MAN, and it is imperative that your child be surrounded by decorations and toys that stimulate, educate and, if needs must, caution and discipline the young mind. No well-equipped nursery room should be in want of the following exhibits :

1. A MORAL MURAL

TO APPRISE THE UNFORMED MIND of the dangers of heathen practices and the innate savagery of the Natural World, and to serve as a warning against travel anywhere south of *Le Touquet*.

2. A MOTIVATING MOBILE
To INSPIRE and instruct.

3. A RIGHTEOUS RELIC
A SOOTHING NIGHTLIGHT in the form of the severed head of John the Baptist to at once instil Christian reverence and aid gentle sleep.

4. AN EDIFYING ALPHABET
TO BE PAINTED as a frieze.

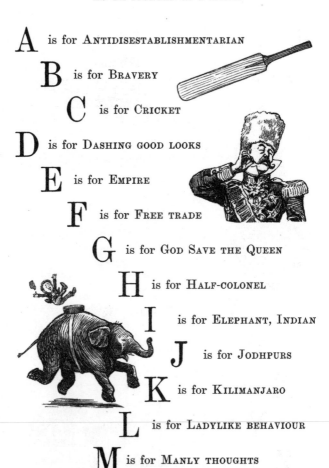

A is for ANTIDISESTABLISHMENTARIAN

B is for BRAVERY

C is for CRICKET

D is for DASHING GOOD LOOKS

E is for EMPIRE

F is for FREE TRADE

G is for GOD SAVE THE QUEEN

H is for HALF-COLONEL

I is for ELEPHANT, INDIAN

J is for JODHPURS

K is for KILIMANJARO

L is for LADYLIKE BEHAVIOUR

M is for MANLY THOUGHTS

N is for Narrow-gauge railway

O is for Obedience

P is for Penal colony

R is for Repeal of the Corn Laws

S is for Silence

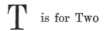

T is for Two

U is for Upper lip

V is for Valet

W is for Whig

X is for Ten

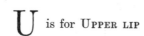

Y is for Youthful vigour

Z is for Zulus, thousands thereof

THE SPLENDID SCIENCE
OF PSYCHOBABBLE

PERHAPS THE MOST IMPRESSIVELY DISTURBED FIGURE of our age is the brilliant alienist Dr Sigmund Freud, a man so clever and so mad that he could have been a headmaster at one of our great public schools. Yet instead of devoting his energies to The Whole Boy, Dr Freud has applied his colossal and febrile brain to the matters of the young mind. For it is the contention of Dr Freud that the character of an adult is formed in the very first few years of life. Indeed, from an infant's first words alone can Dr Freud determine what sort of person the child will grow up to be.

What your child's first words may mean :

"MATER"
Alarming. Son may attempt to have relations with mother and kill father.

"PATER"
Will grow up unhealthily fascinated by the use of the water closet.

"Goo-Goo"
Child has reverted to a childlike state.

"GA-GA"
Individual will grow up to be insane. Ship to Austria for further treatment.

Extracted from Dr Freud's latest clever, albeit upsetting, book *An Oedipus's Garden : The Mother And The Wienerschnitzel*.

BEING A QUESTION PROMPTLY ANSWERED

HOW CAN I GET MY CHILD TO CONSUME VEGETATION ?

MISS FORBES-FROSTE REPLIES : Mealtimes are a time for families to come together, and even very young children take great delight in joining in and doing the same things as the Grown-Ups. Or so people tell me. To be frank, there is far too much hot air talked about what children think or feel or enjoy. Let us be indubitably clear : who cares ? Children almost never have anything interesting to say, are no use whatsoever at *acey-deucey*, and their puny physical statures make them unworthy opponents in the ring. I am personally entirely unconcerned whether they wish to copy the behaviour of adults, other children or, for that matter, a Moroccan houseboy called Ahmed whom grandfather brought back with him from his travels.

I advocate a firm but fair approach to dealing with them, and nowhere is this more important than at the dining table.

Children habitually refuse to eat foods that we know to be advantageous to their health. I wonder how many hundreds of young parents have asked me : "How can I get my darling son to eat his vegetables ?" I give them all the same answer : stuff the vegetables in a clay pipe, hold the child's nose, shove the pipe in his mouth and ignite. It works wonders.

My father caught me fooling around with a carrot as a young girl ; as a punishment, he locked me in the garden shed and would not let me out until I had smoked every root vegetable in there. I learned two valuable lessons : don't get involved with vegetables if you can avoid it ; and try to leave home as soon as humanly possible.

If you really must foist the fruits of the soil upon the fruits of your loins, consider hiding the vegetables under something more toothsome to the child palate, such as Plum Duff, cured meats, Pickled Otter, or perhaps submerge in a glass of Madeira. Alternatively, simply hide the child under the vegetables and remove yourself to the more stimulating dinner company of adults.

CHAPTER 6

POXES, PLAGUES & PANACEAS

BY BARON MUNCHAUSEN VON PROCKSI

—

CHRONIC ARISTOCRAT

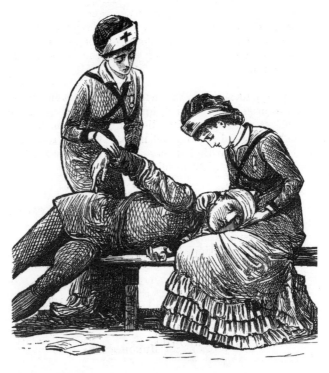

BARON MUNCHAUSEN RECEIVES THE TENDER ATTENTIONS
OF HIS FAVOURITE NURSE, FRAULEIN LÖWENBRÄU

DOCTORS, WITH FEW EXCEPTIONS, ARE SWINE. The nurse, in contrast, her I am liking. Firm, stern, fruity—especially after lights out : that is your ideal nurse. *Fruiternachtnursen*, in my native language. What fine young women they are ; doing excellent work with the sponge and the reassuring smile from Potsdam to Portsmouth.

Herr Doctor, on the other hand... Always wanting to poke, to prod, to lift under things and look there. And worse : often far too slow to dish out the nice medicines to make the head expand and fly far away. Were it not for his selfish hoarding of those clever derivations of the poppy, the adult might avoid him altogether.

The little child, sadly, has no alternative but to visit a medical man every now and again. This is because the little child tends towards sniffles and scrapes, and because his parents can use their superior bulk to compel him to see Herr Doctor. To these young patients I say : be brave. Take your medicine. Comfort yourself with the knowledge that one day you will have children of your own who can distract the doctor while you rifle through his cabinets for some happy pills strong enough to fell a granite rhinoceros.

—LEOPOLD MUNCHAUSEN VON PROCKSI

FIRST PRIZE
MALINGERER OF THE YEAR
1888

MEDAILLE D'OR
GRAND PRIX DE GOUT
1889

WINNER
POORLIEST MAN IN SCHLESWIG-HOLSTEIN
1891

ALARMING AILMENTS

CHILDREN, alas, are prone to illness and general flimsiness of body. Be especially vigilant of the following complaints and seek medical attention without delay if you spot these symptoms in your child :

WHOOPING FACE
> When a cough becomes so violent that the infant face turns inside out. Treat with a balaclava and plenty of iodine.

FROBISHER'S CHEEK
> A distressing condition where a child continually answers back. Apply belt to backside of child three times daily.

FAMILY BUCKET
> An unsightly abdominal protuberance, once thought to be a result of eating undercooked poultry but now understood to be hereditary. Soothe with vienetta ices and scented lemon towels.

SATURDAY NIGHT FEVER
> A disease of the mind where a young child will simulate religious ecstasy in order to be excused Church the following morning. Apply one curate to the affected area.

SCOTSMAN'S WALLET
> An involuntary tightening of the fists. In the most extreme cases, a child can grip with a force equal to that of a small locomotive engine. Treat with whisky.

FIG. 1. COMPLICATIONS
LEFT UNTREATED, A MILD CASE OF FROBISHER'S CHEEK
ADVANCES RAPIDLY TO THE NEXT STAGE OF
THE CONDITION : BEAR-FACED LYING.

FIG. 2. TREATMENT
FILL BUCKET WITH LEECHES. PLACE PATIENT IN BUCKET.

PEAKY OR CHEEKY ? IDENTIFYING THE MOST COMMON RASHES

GIVEN THE INFANT INABILITY to vocalise, diagnosis of illnesses can be tricky—for the layperson. However, the young body has a great deal to tell us via its presentation of rashes. Indeed, to the experienced physician, the hives and eruptions of a child's skin tell a story as well as any words.

Careful study of the examples below will acquaint you with the more common points of difference between the various disorders on offer, sparing you the considerable anguish and embarrassment that result from summoning the doctor to examine a patient who is anything less than half-dead.

THE VON PROCKSI READY RASH-O-RAMA

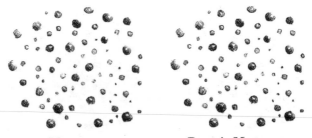

MILKSPOTS
Harmless

DEVIL'S MILKSPOTS
Potentially Fatal

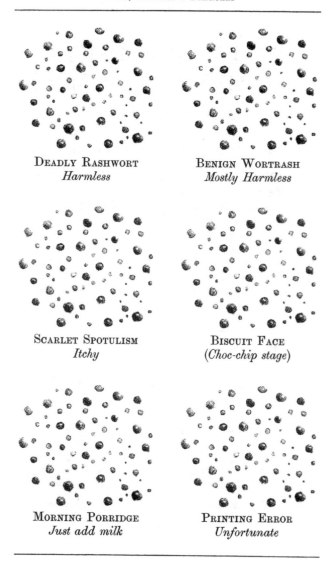

DEADLY RASHWORT
Harmless

BENIGN WORTRASH
Mostly Harmless

SCARLET SPOTULISM
Itchy

BISCUIT FACE
(Choc-chip stage)

MORNING PORRIDGE
Just add milk

PRINTING ERROR
Unfortunate

THE SHAME OF THE UNFUSSY EATER

Picture if you will, gentle reader, a tea party with a collection of mothers and their infants. The jolly meal is to be held at the home of a mater who is quite new to the parish and it is an important opportunity for her to befriend ladies who have children of the same age as her own. Cook has been instructed, the maids have been warned to be on their best behaviour, the handsome young gardener has been told to wear a shorter-than-usual jerkin.

The children are playing happily but silently. The mothers, quite correctly, are taking tea. The hostess has provided an array of cakes and sweet fancies for the child guests. A woodpecker woodpecks engagingly in the garden outside. All appears right with the world.

But social disaster is about to strike...

"Oh dear me no," a mother says as she examines the food on offer. "Young Jerome here simply cannot have anything with egg in it. He is most frightfully allergic."

Another mother gasps and examines the sugary delights. "And I am afraid that this looks as if it may have wheat in it—my darling little Béchamel is absolutely unable to stomach grains of any description."

Not to be outdone, a third chimes : "My precious Timmytomkins ! Step away from that scone this instant. It may conceivably have been in contact with dairy products at some point during the preparation process. Or seeds, or lint, or something. Are you trying to murder my child, you wicked harridan ?"

"I'm sorry. I'm so sorry," the hostess sobs. "My little boy Jack enjoys almost all foods and does not seem to be allergic to anything. Forgive me. Please, please forgive me."

The mothers turn their gaze upon the hostess, some angry, some appalled, others merely pitying. Of all the shameful, wretched errors ! To raise a child without perpetually brandishing a food allergy from which it might conceivably suffer ! Implying that it is able to digest everyday foodstuffs—like a common guttersnipe ! This mother quite evidently does not love her child.

A child without a food intolerance is as naked and alone in the world as the most pathetic orphan. As a society, we ought to tolerate everything except tolerance. If you love your child, invent an allergy today.

FIG. 1. PINCER MOVEMENT
Paul, the man-eating lobster, ably assists a doting father with his latest round of seafood aversion therapy.

VACCINATION : THE CLEVEREST INVENTION SINCE TROUSERS

ALL ACROSS EUROPE, astonishing advances in the field of immunisation are underway. In Germany, the brilliant Herr Robert Koch, Professor of Hygiene at the University of Berlin, has developed a vaccine for tuberculosis. Although there is no equivalent Chair of Hygiene at the Sorbonne, Paris being a filthy city, Louis Pasteur toils day and night in his *Laboratoire Garnier* to slay the beast rabies. In the Mystic East, the wily Japanese Kitasato Shibasaburo is locked in a fight to the death with bubonic plague. And closer to home, Mrs Edith Brote of Cheam is convinced her experiments may one day rid her cabbages of greenfly ; and who is to say that human urine will not turn out to be a powerful insect repellent ?

Babies, like cabbages, can benefit from early exposure to small doses of pestilent, nasty or otherwise un-Christian germs, the better to burnish their breastplate for life's battles ahead. Consider bringing your child into contact with controlled amounts of :

MEASLES	RED-HEADED CHILDREN
FRECKLES	BOVINE BLISTERS
BLACK DEATH	BLACK SHEEP
PEOPLE FROM HULL	CHICKEN CHOLERA
POXES, VARIOUS	CHICKEN CHASSEUR

REMEMBER : a little pain now may save a deal of misery later ; or should at least give the patient valuable practice in being miserable ahead of their teenage years.

FIG. 1. THE VACCINATED CHILD
Noble bearing. Rich in moral fibre.

FIG. 2. THE UN-VACCINATED CHILD
Suffers from an acute case of Monkey Shoulder.
Lives in a Barrel. Probably on fire.

ALTERNATIVE MEDICINE : LAST REFUGE OF THE HOPELESS

UNSURE ABOUT THE EFFICACY OF MEDICAL SCIENCE ? Frightened of doctors ? Dull of wit ? Do not belabour your brain with the cold unfeeling brutality of facts and reason ; bask instead on the sunlit uplands of the new alternative medicine.

All over Britain, the clever techniques of setting things on fire, sniffing them, inserting them into oneself or simply gargling with solutions of debatable provenance are restoring mothers and their ailing babes to the fullest bloom of health.

With conventional medical practitioners being too busy, too brusque or too possessing of intimidating whiskers, many ordinary people now prefer to give the family doctor a wide berth.

Rather than journey several miles to a surgery and sit there in bafflement while a well-educated old gentleman barks orders at them, they are choosing to rely on pagan, foreign or otherwise enigmatic techniques to treat their young.

Methods include homeo-pathic dilutional deviousness, whose wonders will soon make head colds a thing of the past. If your child is beginning to sneeze and cough, add two drops of lavender oil to a nearby lake and make the child drink the lake. By morning, the

Fig. 1. *The Good Doctor :*
Less concerned with bedside
manner than legside technique.

Fig. 2. Full of drinky goodness. And fish.

chest will be completely cleared—although the lake may need further dredging in its reediest areas.

If your child has measles, do not waste your time trying to seek advice from a doctor : Aromatic Therapy using unguents of the quintessence is your surest solution. Boil up a pair of socks with rhubarb and custard and have the patient inhale the vapours. You should notice an improvement almost immediately. In extreme cases, hypnotise the child by waving one of the socks in front of its face before boiling.

Children often get into scrapes or suffer minor scratches during play. If a child, for example, were to chop its limbs off with an axe during a rumbustious session of amusement in the garden or medieval armoury, do not look to the hidebound solutions of 'traditional' medicine. Simply rub St John's Wort on to the affected area and the arms and legs will grow back within a day or two.

From curing cholera with healing hands to overturning vampirism with the application of gooseberry-scented oils, there is nothing that cannot be accomplished with a few natural herbs, some candles and a healthy dose of blind, mindless faith.

DOCTORING FOR THE KEEN AMATEUR

FOR THOSE MALADIES which present no outward signs, a more subtle diagnosis may be needed. Examine various aspects of the invalid's demeanour in turn, and assess each as might a medical orderly or physician.

1. COLOUR

FIRST CONSIDER the hue and pallor of the skin and score the sickling child accordingly.

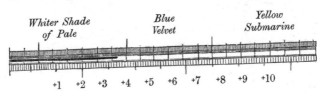

Whiter Shade of Pale   *Blue Velvet*   *Yellow Submarine*

+1   +2   +3   +4   +5   +6   +7   +8   +9   +10

Turn next to the outer extremities. Is your patient :

GREEN-FINGERED	+2 *points*
RED-HANDED	+3 *points*
BROWN-NOSED	+4 *points*
GENERALLY STAINED OF CHARACTER	+5 *points*

2. CARDIAC RHYTHM

USING A POCKETWATCH or chronometer, tally the number of heartbeats within a given time period : [1]

0-60 (-1)   61-90 (+1)   91-99 (+2)   100-200 (+3)

---

[1] Figures obtained with the aid of a sundial must be rounded to the nearest pedestal.

3. TEMPERATURE

PLACE YOUR HAND on the patient's brow and consider the heat emitting therefrom. Gloves should be worn in cases of contagion or general grubbiness.

White Hot (+3)   *Red Hot* (+2)   *Hot Rod* (-1)   *Cold Fish* (+1)

4. COMPULSIONS

IS THE CHILD suffering from any of the following ?

INVOLUNTARY VOLUNTARISM (+2)   UNWITTING WITTICISM (+3)   LYCANTHROPY (+6)

5. EXPULSIONS

HAS THE PATIENT brought forth any of the following ?

DISHONOURABLE DISCHARGE (+3)
VILE BILE (+4)
FUR BALLS (+6)

6. CONCLUSIONS

BASED ON THE EVIDENCE THUS OBTAINED, your child is almost certainly suffering from a case of :

0-5 *points*	POOR ARITHMETIC
6-19 *points*	ACUTE OBTUSENESS
20-29 *points*	OBSESSIVE REPULSIVE DISORDER
30-35 *points*	BISHOP'S FINGER
99-801 *points*	TOTAL ECLIPSE OF THE HEART

BEING A QUESTION PROMPTLY ANSWERED

HELP ! MY BABY IS MAKING AN UPSETTING RACKET. WHAT IS THE MATTER WITH IT ?

A FUSSY, SCREAMING, GRIPING BABY is almost invariably attributable to one of two factors. Diagnose it thus :

—Baby crying for extended periods ?
—Stretching and writhing uncomfortably ?
—Vomiting ?
—Irritability ?

The most likely explanation is COLIC.

—Baby crying out vile slurs in Latin ?
—Head revolving on neck ?
—Projectile-vomiting green bile ?
—Eyes turning black and furniture flying around room ?

The most likely explanation is DEMONIC POSSESSION.

Treat either condition with soothing sounds, gentle rocking and exorcism. In older children, look out for signs of early sexual maturity, not wanting to go to Evensong or levitation. These usually speak to some sort of malevolent interference from the spirit world, or a lazy governess.

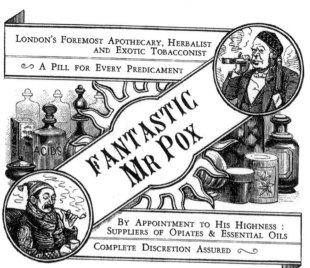

LONDON'S FOREMOST APOTHECARY, HERBALIST AND EXOTIC TOBACCONIST

A PILL FOR EVERY PREDICAMENT

FANTASTIC MR POX

BY APPOINTMENT TO HIS HIGHNESS : SUPPLIERS OF OPIATES & ESSENTIAL OILS

COMPLETE DISCRETION ASSURED

MESSRS BERNERS LEE AND WALES'

SICKIPEDIA

ALL THE WORLD'S ILLNESSES AT THE TURN OF A PAGE

UPDATED DAILY BY AMATEURS

FULL LIST OF ALL ACHES PAINS ILLS COUGHS CARES HURTS WARTS SPITS SPOTS TICKS AND POCKS

FOR EVERY MINOR SYMPTOM, A HIDEOUS AILMENT PROMISED!

FREE COPY OF 'DRESS TO IMPRESS—THE ART OF BANDAGING AND BADINAGE' WITH EVERY ORDER

CHAPTER 7

FATHERHOOD

BY MR REGGIE SHIRKER
—

ACTING DIRECTOR,
HENLEY INSTITUTE FOR
PATRICIAN STUDIES

CULTIVATING THE ART OF BENIGN NEGLECT

Hot flushes, wild fluctuations in appetite, feelings of despair, exhaustion and a sense of being overwhelmed ? The weeks following the birth of a child can be extremely trying for a new father.

Even a most summary perusal of the literature about birth and childcare shows it to focus almost exclusively upon the duties of the mother. And quite right too. However, some men are inspired to become involved in looking after a baby or child, and there is no reason why the modern gentleman should not occasionally ring for a nursemaid to change the baby, smile at the child once in a while or even take an interest in its development prior to the traditional first formal introduction at the age of twenty-one.

Remember : it is your child as much as your wife's (assuming nothing scandalous has occurred) and it is quite acceptable to assist, in a supervisory capacity of course, in its upbringing.

—R. Shirker

SOME WORDS OF ADVICE FOR A NEW PATER UPON THE BIRTH OF A BOY

HEARTIEST CONGRATULATIONS ! For some, paterhood can be a most rewarding experience, and there is much to look forward to with your son. Teaching your boy to play cricket, wear a hat, grow lamb-chop whiskers, smoke a cigar, invade a country or run a cotton mill can be most enriching, and you will no doubt be eager to shape him into exactly the sort of fellow you would have liked to have been yourself. Whether he cares for it or not.

Aside from passing on all you have learned as the boy develops, there are two primary duties for a papa. The first is discipline, which we shall discuss shortly. So put that belt down for now, pater ! The second is the choosing and purchase of a perambulator or baby carriage.

Because these machines can be both technologically advanced and tricksy to operate, it falls upon the man of the house to select one. Look for a vehicle that is made of cast iron, coal-fired if your budget permits, and ideally weighing about six to eight hundredweight. This will ensure durability, and that your wife gets a good bit of exercise if she has to carry it on to an omnibus.

SOME WORDS OF ADVICE FOR A NEW PATER UPON THE BIRTH OF A GIRL

Commiserations.

THE WELL-IGNORED CHILD IS THE FATHER OF THE SUCCESSFUL MAN

OBSERVE how some of the greatest figures of our age were comprehensively disregarded by their mothers and fathers—and how over-attentive parenting produced some of the est monsters...

W.G. GRACE—father did not speak to the master batsman until he was nine.

CHARLES DICKENS—mother shut him in coal cellar with pen and notepaper until he was tall enough to climb out (aged seventeen).

BENJAMIN DISRAELI—until the age of thirty, whenever the great parliamentarian spoke, his mother would say : "Can anyone hear an annoying whining noise ?"

ISAMBARD KINGDOM BRUNEL—parents refused to speak to him until he had constructed Clifton Suspension Bridge. Sadly they died before it was completed, or indeed even planned.

———

JACK THE RIPPER—it is believed that his father probably joined him in games of chess, quoits or shove-ha'penny.

MARY ANN COTTON—mother of the multiple murderess encouraged her to chatter away quite brazenly.

THOMAS DE QUINCEY—the vile literary figure was known to be on cordial terms with both parents even as a youngster.

NED KELLY—parents allowed him to speak when not spoken to—*and in Australian, at that.*

FIG. 1.
'LA-LA-LA-LA-LA-LA'
A FATHER WITH HIS CHILD'S
BEST INTERESTS AT HEART

BONDING FOR BEGINNERS

UNTIL SCIENCE ADVANCES FURTHER, spending time with one's children remains an unavoidable fact of fatherhood. Sadly, as most fathers soon discover, the average child is not up to much when it comes to the main diversions that occupy a man's recreational hours : shooting pheasant, seducing servants and touring the local distilleries. Even the thrill of parting a toddler from his allowance at the card table begins to wane after the third or fourth child.

Happily, the Henley Institute for Patrician Studies has recently devised a number of alternative activities which furnish greater scope for paterno-pipsqueak collaboration.

AMATEUR ACROBATICS
(AGES 0-3)

ADVANTAGES :
Employment opportunities
in circus

DISADVANTAGES :
May grow up into
Bearded Lady

RELATED PURSUITS :
Housebreaking, Catburglary

FISHING (AGES 1-5)

ADVANTAGES :
More substantial bait should attract larger pike

DISADVANTAGES :
Having to explain to wife why her first-born is now
in belly of said pike

RELATED PURSUITS :
Heir Coursing, Peer Stalking

SERVANT RACING (AGES 2-6)

ADVANTAGES :
Keeps one's staff on their toes

DISADVANTAGES :
Risk of upset if favourite footman pulls up lame
and has to be put down

RELATED PURSUITS :
Butler Baiting, Governess Grappling

MAKING STUFFED TOYS (AGES 3-6)

ADVANTAGES :
Commemorates well-loved family pet

DISADVANTAGES :
Requires the death of well-loved family pet

RELATED PURSUITS :
Galvanic Reanimation, Zombie Rustling

CRIME & PUNISHMENT : DISCIPLINE FOR DADDIES

MATRIARCHAL SOCIETIES—the spotted hyena, the Italian—tend towards unruliness. And while ladies are beyond dispute doing splendid work in the fields of giving birth, producing milk and choosing soft fabrics to adorn the youngster's bedroom, discipline remains the ultimate responsibility of the pater.

However, fathers in all strata of society know how wearying it can be to return home from a day of work—whether at a mill, owning a mill, or pontificating in a university about John Stuart Mill—to be assailed with a child's wheedling demands before one has even got one's coat off and a restorative half-pint of gin down the happy-sluice.

Children respond well to firm commands and consistency, but are alarmed by sudden movements, be they physical or ethical. If a child asks you for permission to do something, or requests that you mediate in a dispute, the proper hierarchy of response is :

a) ask your Mater
b) ask Cook (if the enquiry is related to comestibles)
c) ask the Editor of *The Times* in a formal letter

If none of these yields a definitive answer, you may be forced to make a decision yourself. Do not be alarmed. With luck, you will be back at work or asleep in your study under the newspaper before the full hideous consequences of allowing young Bartholomew to ride his bi-cycle in the drawing room wreak havoc upon your household—and your wife's shredded nerves.

As to disciplining a child, while you should not be reticent in using the full range of sanctions at your disposal, be aware that the punishment ought to be commensurate with the crime. A mild case of cheeking might be punished by being sent to bed early, or being denied pudding, but it would not be appropriate to send your child off for a spell in the Foreign Legion, at least not until the second offence.

Transportation to Australia should be a last resort, except in the case of a persistently untidied bedroom.

If a child refuses to say its prayers, excommunication can be a cost-effective solution, and has the additional benefit of ensuring that you will not have to attend any more of the little heretic's nativity plays.

Like almost anything in life, the disciplinary aspects of parenthood are best enjoyed from a safe distance, ideally with someone else doing much of the gruelling spadework. Be firm, be fair, and do not let your children trap you into a story you cannot change later once your wife becomes involved.

FIG. 1. THE OTHER KIND OF DISCIPLINE FOR DADDIES

MOW MONEY
MOW PROBLEMS

GIVING A CHILD A WEEKLY STIPEND in exchange for the performance of some simple chores can teach the value of money—and also provide a household with an easy source of cheap labour.

Adherence to a strict pricing chart is important if you are to avoid the sort of wage inflation that has ruined the profit margin in the textile industry.

ONE FARTHING—cutting of grass on East Lawn (one farthing bonus if lawn is larger than one acre ; one additional farthing if child supplies own scissors).

ONE HALFPENNY—washing, waxing, polishing and valeting locomotive engine of the Flying Scotsman.

ONE HALFPENNY—washing the dishes after a dinner attended by company. One extra farthing if meal was more than twenty-seven courses.

ONE PENNY—pouring papa an acceptably generous drink, trimming cigar, running down to bookmaker's and other morally improving tasks.

ONE SHILLING—dressing up as father, going to his place of employment for a week and fulfilling professional duties in his stead. One penny if undetected ; one further penny if pater is in Army, Church, government.

REMEMBER : children are wily, and you should never hand over cash up front. If possible, try to pay with an I.O.U. or negotiate to offset 'pocket monies' against future board and lodging costs incurred by yourself in the upkeep of the child.

BEING A QUESTION PROMPTLY ANSWERED

HOW OFTEN OUGHT ONE TO SEE ONE'S CHILD ?

FOR LONG PERIODS OF ENGLISH HISTORY, and some would say that those were simpler, happier times, a papa's responsibilities towards his offspring were clearly defined within rather narrow boundaries. He would fulfil his sole duty towards the youngster on the eve of the boy's first day at public school, when he would summon his son to the study and offer him the sound advice that he had received from his own father as a child going off to board : "Keep your bowels open and your mouth shut."

This modest degree of interaction seemed to work perfectly well for generations of Englishmen, who were happy to leave the bringing up of children to their womenfolk while they got on with the serious business of soldiering, exploration and sticking it up the noses of their European neighbours.

However, it is a fact of modern life that everywhere one turns, one sees women trying to behave like men, men trying to behave like women and, in many parts of the North, men and women simply behaving like animals. And we at the Henley Institute for Patrician Studies are receiving an increasing number of telegrams and personal visits from gentlemen who are concerned that they are insufficiently involved in the bringing up of their children.

We stress to them in the clearest possible terms that to become more involved would not make them unmanly, soppy, meddling little girlie-men, no matter what others may say. The Institute is a broad church, and we are not here to pass judgement, so long as a client pays his bill in a timely fashion. We are more than happy to offer advice upon how to increase the amount of time you spend with your progeny, be it meeting with the child in your library for a stern talking-to every Whitsun ; or the less hidebound technique of acknowledging him or her with a raised eyebrow over the devilled kidneys once in a while.

If you so wish, do not feel embarrassed to take an active role in parenting on a monthly or even weekly basis. For good or ill, the days when speaking to one's offspring was a sign of moral enfeeblitude have long past. The Henley Institute for Patrician Studies, however, accepts no responsibility in the event of a child becoming clingy ; and bonding is undertaken at your own risk.

As with everything related to parenting there is no right or wrong answer, only that which you and your wife feel comfortable droning on about to anybody who will listen. Therefore we say : "Fathers of England—meet your children."

OLD FATHER'S

QUALITY TIMER

ENSURE YOUR CHILD RECEIVES THE CORRECT AMOUNT OF ATTENTION —AND NOT A SECOND MORE !

PRECISION PARENTING GUARANTEED

PREPARE THE PERFECT EGGHEAD

5 minutes—Hard-boiled
3 minutes—Soft in the head
4½ minutes—Just Right !

FOUNDING MEMBER OF THE WORSHIPFUL ORDER OF CLOCKWATCHERS AND WIND-UP MERCHANTS

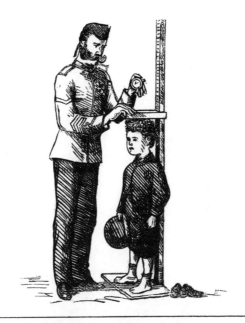

CHAPTER 8

FROM INFANCY
TO INFANTRY

BY LT.-COL. SIR WINSTON STIFF

—

GAY HUSSAR

"NOT TONIGHT, JOSEPH"

YOUR LITTLE SOLDIER has fought a successful campaign against the arduous opponent that is babyhood. Teething, weaning, talking and basic table manners have all fallen to his bow and arrow. Sitting up straight and polishing his own shoes hold no fear. He has even learned to bayonet a sister's favoured dolly. Now an even more gruelling crusade lies ahead : the battle of life.

Will your child be a dashing hero upon his white charger, riding into the fray armed with the simple sword of truth, the trusty shield of British fair play, the sturdy breastplate of the L.B.W. law and the plumed helmet of social superiority ? Or will he cower at the back with the weeds, the do-gooders and the Continentals ?

Many tactical decisions lie ahead and he will need your wise counsel. From childhood parties to school and the world of work, the young Englishman's journey is one to be undertaken stoutly, honourably and with due care and attention to wearing the right sort of socks. Let us march on together.

Stiff

YOUTH'S MILESTONES AND HOW TO APPROACH THEM

JUST AS A SOLIDER is not a true warrior until he has been garrisoned in Cyprus and visited some serious unpleasantness upon the unfortunate citizenry, a boy cannot be called a young man until he has undergone a few important rites of passage.

The first is saying goodbye to a beloved childhood toy. Be it a teddy bear, a pretty bonnet, a small-bore shotgun or a treasured copy of the *Aeneid*, no man can progress on life's journey if he is encumbered by possessions. I learned this from a Buddhist monk I once assaulted outside a haberdasher's in Mandalay.

Some particularly sentimental children form attachments not just to a chattel but to a favourite servant. My brother had enormous trouble with his two younger sons on just this matter : little Cuthbert was inordinately fond of his comfort valet, while it was quite impossible to get Rufus to fall asleep unless he had his beloved smelly, ratty old footman upon which to chew. My brother Rudolph was always far too soft ; and if person or persons unknown had not had the presence of mind to have the two elderly domestics taken away by the constabulary after treasured family heirlooms were found underneath their beds, my nephews might have gone up to Oxford still clutching their cherished, decrepit retainers.

Award decorations for good soldiering. The non-commissioned toddler's first successful unaccompanied expedition to the lavatory ought to be rewarded with a standing chit for permission to visit that room without need for repeated entreaty. Particularly correct use of the water closet might be encouraged by the promise of access to the inside facilities in the colder months ; or at least being allowed some form of lamp on the one-mile trek to the outdoor privy, and a weapon if the outhouse is situated in hostile territory.

A child's first kill is also a significant milestone. Be it a hare, a stag, a rare owl or a Prussian, it is imperative that the day be marked with a celebration. Ensure that the most senior, and most frightening, surviving family member is the one to administer the blooding. And note well the reaction of the child ; it can provide many clues as to the youngster's mettle. As soon as I saw my great-niece Clarissa's shameful sobbing after having a bucket of dead pheasant emptied over her head, I said to myself : "That is the most pathetic six-year-old girl I have ever seen." Sure enough, she amounted to very little in adult life, although she did found a charity dedicated to the protection of wild birds.

FIG. 1. THE SECURITY SERVANT. WASH AT YOUR PERIL.

SETTING YOUR CHILD UPON THE RIGHT PATH

FATHERHOOD OPENS UP a world of opportunities for living vicariously through the achievements of one's children. As you ponder whether your son will go on to captain England at cricket, become a military man of standing, a politician of great renown or the discoverer of a new type of dessert wine, employ this simple chart to determine the career path your boy should follow.

I.
BEING A CHART TO DETERMINE A BOY'S F.L.O.W. (FUTURE LIFE OR WORK)

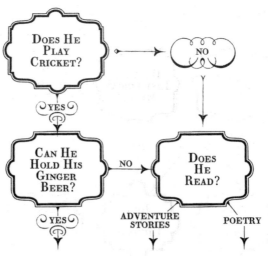

—Pray go with the F.L.O.W. to the facing page—

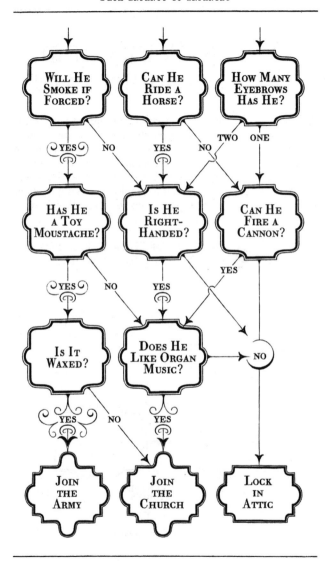

II.
BEING A CHART TO DETERMINE THE
PROSPECTS OF A FEMALE CHILD

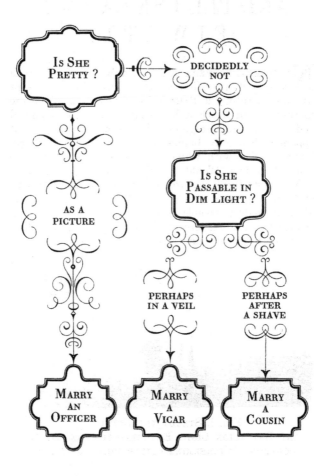

IS SHE PRETTY?

DECIDEDLY NOT

IS SHE PASSABLE IN DIM LIGHT?

AS A PICTURE

PERHAPS IN A VEIL

PERHAPS AFTER A SHAVE

MARRY AN OFFICER

MARRY A VICAR

MARRY A COUSIN

IT'S MY PARTY
AND I'LL USE CANNON
IF I WANT TO

No MILITARY OPERATION is planned with as much care and attention as the successful children's party. Generally, the British Army is careful to engage in conflicts in which it has a significant technological and strategic advantage over its opponent ; and if that opponent has only blades of grass or an amusingly knobbly stick with which to defend himself, then so much the better. Would that this were the case here.

You might think that you, as a full-grown adult human with the resources of a decent-sized household at your disposal, ought to be able to conduct a defensive campaign against an invading force of children's party guests. This would be to gravely underestimate your foe.

Fig. 1. Steady the Buffet !
2nd Battalion Light Entertainers prepare to confront Wilhelmina's sixth birthday party

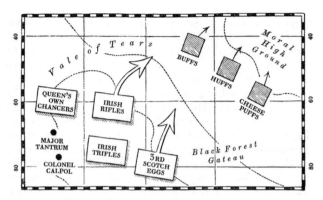

FIG. 2. OPERATION 'DESSERT STORM'

There is no more formidable guerrilla adversary than a company of five-year-olds at a birthday party : its movement is fluid, its energy overpowering, its shrieking vicious. The infant party paramilitary has mastered weaponry and techniques from closed-formation hurtful giggling to stuffing jam sandwiches down the side of a favourite armchair ; and an especially snotty brigade can reduce a poorly defended drawing room or library to matchwood in minutes. They are nimble, they are merciless and they get overtired easily.

From the moment the enemy engages, he must be distracted constantly. Deploy Magicians early. Pepper the foe with balloon animals. Do not allow him to get hold of sugary drinks. If there is enough in your war chest, consider the importation of mercenaries drawn from the sinister underworld of Children's Entertainment to befuddle and delight the beastly little revellers for a few minutes while you regroup in the study with smelling salts and a stiff drink.

However, no matter how well you have prepared, it is certain that you will be over-run by mid-afternoon.

This is the time to deploy your shock troops : CLOWNS. Even the most well-drilled party unit can be reduced to silence if faced by a Clown of sufficient scariness. As with all military manoeuvres, the element of surprise is key. Isolate the enemy officers or kingpins—perhaps when one is helping himself to more lemonade at the refreshment table. Have Clown leap out from behind an armoire, bookcase or stuffed tiger. Frighten thoroughly. Panic should spread through the ranks. Short of Furrberising—the controversial technique of controlled battle-crying developed by Field Marshall Nils van der Furrber—this Pennywising branch of psychological warfare is considered the most effective weapon in the conflict against unruly children known to military science.

FIG. 3. CLOWN DOWN

By four o'clock, if you have acceded to the enemy's every demand for the spoils of war—sickly drinks and cake—it may be possible to negotiate a settlement and withdrawal. Home time may yet come, but by heaven it comes at a price.

An extravagantly-filled 'goody-bag' is your only hope of parleying a ceasefire. Spare no expense ; and know well that these piratical little invaders communicate about the relative splendour of party booty. If they discover your goody-bag to be lighter than the one received at the recent festivities of young Persephone at number 42, terrible will be their wrath, and there will be no place on earth for you to hide. Give thanks that your son or daughter has but one birthday per annum, and if you have more than one child, may God help you.

FIG. 4. PLUNDER OR CHUNDER

BEING A QUESTION PROMPTLY ANSWERED

CAN ONE LEARN ANYTHING ABOUT PARENTING FROM THE LOWER RANKS ?

WITH THEIR DEVIL-MAY-CARE APPROACH to dentistry and personal hygiene, their enthusiastic sexual appetites and their marvellous natural sense of rhythm, the English working classes indubitably know how to drink deep of life's heady brew.

And when he is not in the jolly old public house having a pint of beer, playing at football under one code or another, or singing a jaunty song outside a music hall on the Old Kent Road, the working-class man's thoughts turn immediately to hopping on top of his working-class wife and getting her in the family way without further ado.

It is quite common for working-class men and women—who marry in broadly similar ceremonies to ours—to have as many as three dozen children. The average working-class girl aims to be pregnant for approximately forty-four years of her life, starting as soon as she is old enough to cook her own breakfast and not letting up from the production of babies until she is old and grey and the size of a small wardrobe.

The working-class anatomy is essentially identical to our own, although the females have slightly larger ears and the males cannot pronounce the letter T. Their family lives are characterised by a great many children, being rather noisy and a fondness for dangerous pets. Contrary to some scurrilous reports in the more breathless of the women's papers, the working class do NOT eat their own young, or at least not unless they have lost a great deal of money betting on dog racing.

One notable consequence of working-class folk wisdom is their propensity to breed early in life, a much more sensible course of action than the middle classes' dubious policy of waiting until the woman is very old or even actually deceased before attempting her first pregnancy. Thus the working-class mother has a great deal more energy and vim, and can also share clothes with her offspring.

In addition, the working-class mother is generally fonder of spending time with her child because she is not at all eager 'to return to work' ; and nor would you be, gentle reader, if you worked in a manure factory rather than in a charming little *boutique*.

Although his coat may be threadbare and his grasp of poetry and politics tenuous at best, the working-class man is nevertheless the master of all he surveys in his own home (unless one of the landowning classes decides to turn his home into a tennis court) and it is in the area of family discipline that his most impressive work is done. Not for the working-class man the dinner-table debates about the Suffragist movement, the rights of child chimney sweeps or whether little Thomasina ought to be allowed to roll hoops with that rather forward girl next door : he rules with an iron fist, and if an argument is best settled by going out on the drink for a few weeks and becoming press-ganged into the Navy as a result, he is more than happy to make his point in that manner.

All hail the splendid spirit of the working class and their multitudinous offspring !

PARENTING IN THE FUTURE

BY MR HUBERT BUNSEN-BURNER
—
GENTLEMAN SCIENTIST & PROGNOSTICATOR

THE FUTURE IS BRIGHT ;
THE FUTURE IS WATERY ORANGE CORDIAL

AFTERWORD

According to my calculations and experiments, parenting will become four times easier by the year 1954 ; and by the second decade of the twenty-first century, the production and care of children will be so efficient and simple that parents will be able to do it standing on their heads—literally, if they so wish.

Look around you, dear reader, and see technological cleverness everywhere helping parents Bring Up Baby, including sophisticated techniques to communicate with baby via semaphore, electric pajamas, and multitudinous ingenious machines for feeding, cleaning and disciplining a child. Join me in daring to wonder at the march of progress and how far mankind might advance.

In a recent experiment involving a mangle, a brush, a child's dolly, a *bain-marie* at the right temperature, shavings of the wonderful metal aluminium, a pocket watch and Sarah-Jane, the young girl who helps my sister with childcare duties on Wednesday when Nanny has her day off, I was able to make an astonishing finding. I should very much like to tell you about it.

I heated the pocket watch in the water and began— very gradually—to add the aluminium to it. Soon I had a light but strong, stable liquid constituted of molten metal, cogs, springs, the hands of the watch and a bit of sausage that fell in from the sandwich I was eating, whose effects I am confident to discount. In the resultant chronological soup was contained the future of metallurgy, childcare and time travel itself.

For meanwhile, I had set Sarah-Jane to work in my laboratory, washing and running some clothes through the mangle, sweeping the floor, tidying, &c., all the while holding and talking to the dolly (it being impractical to use a real child, because my sister would not lend me one) in order to simulate the daily life of the put-upon young mother. I told the girl that if I had finished my experiments before she finished her cleaning duties, I would give her an informative lecture (at no charge to herself) on the properties of the marvellous new metallic compound *Watchtominium* and its applications in domestic household management. The girl's productivity increased dramatically and she completed her work in less than half the normal time.

Taking this early success for *Watchtominium* and extrapolating therefrom, I have proved that within a few decades it will be possible to build domestic servants and child-carers from the metal ; and that the housemaid of tomorrow will surely perform her duties with such alacrity and vigour that she would actually be able to clean my laboratory before I asked her to do so, effectively meaning that she might disappear into the very sands of time itself. To this I attribute Sarah-Jane's failure to present herself at my laboratory since the first experiment.

Also on the subject of time, the ever-increasing speed at which man in the year 1896 can produce goods has profound implications. There is no scientific reason that humans should not apply this splendid new spirit of mechanised competence to the more effective production of new, smaller humans. By the third millennium, we will see pregnancy become so efficient that gestation periods for a human child may be as short as a week or two. Indeed it may be that the woman of the future will have

THE AUTO-DIDACT OR 'HANNIBAL LECTURER':
DESIGN FOR A MECHANICAL TEACHING AID
CAST FROM PUREST WATCHTOMINIUM

relations with her husband, a short rest and something nutritious to eat, and then give birth to a perfectly healthy baby in time for a jaunty sailing expedition at the weekend. This will mean that families, especially those of the middle classes, will grow to number forty or fifty children per marriage, ensuring that England remains firmly atop the world in commerce, Empire and sporting endeavour, through sheer weight of numbers if nothing else.

Children, likewise, will age more quickly, so that by the first or second decade of the new millennium, the future child of, say, six years old will already have attended university, become disillusioned with its career, taken up golf and perhaps run off with its secretary. Parenting this precocious new generation will be a matter of trifling ease, although if progress continues to advance with the alacrity I estimate, children will quite soon have become older than their parents.

This may sound distressing, but parents of the future need not worry : not only will their superannuated sons and daughters be making important contributions to the household income by becoming gainfully employed from the age of two, but the accelerated offspring will also be able to read all the necessary books about childcare for themselves, thus allowing their parents to get on with pastimes that are far more relaxing and enjoyable. And should these auto-parenting children of the future need guidance, I am certain that the advice contained in this particular little volume will be as relevant in centuries to come as it is in 1896.

So, then, parents of today and children of tomorrow : forward into the glorious future with GIN & JUICE.

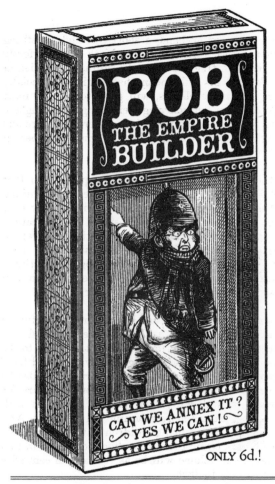

IGNATIUS PERCIVAL'S TOPICAL TOY EMPORIUM

STOCKISTS OF : Brickbats || Catapults & Hawarden Kites
Paper Tigers || Tinpot Generals || Puppet Kings & Queens
Sideshows || Diversions || Machinations & Flags of Convenience

Always remember : a British Protectorate is for LIFE, not just for CHRISTMAS

FURTHER READING

GIN & JUICE—THE COCKTAIL COMPANION
Garnons & Williams (Forward Press, 1895)

TIN & SLUICE—FATHERHOOD THE CORNISH WAY
Charles Atyeo (Cider Press, 1890)

DJINN & JEWS—PARENTING IN THE LEVANT
Ebenezer Hornbuckle (Trouser Press, 1896)

THE CHARGE OF THE LIGHT-FINGERED BRIGADE—
PERFECT PARTY PLANNING FOR PARENTS
Lord Cardigan (Balaclava Books, 1854)

AU PAIR DE LA LUNE—ADVENTURES IN SLAVERY
Patrice Pantoufle (Editions de la Rue, 1833)

SPANKS FOR PRANKS—A NANNY FONDLY REMEMBERS
Nanny Fanny Fanlight (Striking Publications, 1888)

A ROOM WITHOUT A VIEW—INFANT IN THE ATTIC
M. Ivory (Books for Nooks, 1896)

WEREWOLF OR POODLE?—CHOOSING A SUITABLE PET
Ezekiel Boniface (Full Moon Press, 1891)

RUMMY MUMMY
Elizabeth Cougar (Gin Lane, 1751)

MOTHERING HEIGHTS
E. Brontë (Chick Lit., 1847)

GIN & JUICE
THE VICTORIAN GUIDE TO PARENTING

First published 2012 by
Bloomsbury Publishing Plc
50 Bedford Square
London WC1B 3DP
www.bloomsbury.com

Copyright © Alan Tyers and Beach
www.tyersandbeach.com

ISBN 978 1 4088 2434 4

A CIP catalogue record for this book is available from
the British Library.

This book is produced using paper that is made from wood grown in
managed, sustainable forests. It is natural, renewable and recyclable.
The logging and manufacturing processes conform to the
environmental regulations of the country of origin.

10 9 8 7 6 5 4 3 2 1

Typeset in Gin Modern.
Printed in Great Britain by Clays Ltd, St Ives Plc.